For beloved Wolf 832F

Myth & Magic: An Enchanted Fantasy Coloring Book
by Kinuko Y. Craft

Published by Amber Lotus Publishing
PO Box 11329, Portland, OR 97211-0329

Copyright © 2016 Amber Lotus Publishing. www.amberlotus.com
Artwork copyright © 2016 Kinuko Y. Craft. www.kycraft.com
All rights reserved.
No part of this document may be reproduced or transmitted in any form
or by any means, electronic, mechanical, photocopying, recording, or otherwise,
without prior written permission from the artist. Printed in the United States of America.

Designed by Leslie Gignilliat-Day

FIRST EDITION

ISBN: 978-1-63136-243-9
10 9 8 7 6 5 4 3 2 1

Myth & Magic
A COLORING BOOK BY KINUKO Y. CRAFT

Painting is my language, my poetry, my therapy, my meditation, my passion—it's everything. It is me. It is who I am. When I look at paintings created by the masters of the Italian Renaissance, I am filled with the presence of the artist—as if the artist's energy is still there, somehow captured in the pigment. The color and light dazzle and enchant me, propelling me to another time and place with a feeling of eternity.

When I was invited to create a coloring book of line drawings, I was excited to share my work yet felt the challenge of working without my beloved paint—the dazzling full spectrum of color and pure pigments. I long to experience the tactile, sensual energy of direct contact between my hand, the paint, and the surface. I want to convey all the emotion of each illustration to its fullest expression. How would I achieve that without paint?

Yet after creating the first few sketches, I delighted in the idea that you and I will craft a masterpiece together. So, please, lose yourself in stories of mythic beings, heroines, fairy princesses, and enchanted landscapes as you imbue each illustration with jewel-like tones or subtle hues to make it your own. My line compositions are an invitation for you to fall in love with color.

Artists don't create as a gift to others: they create for themselves because it fulfills some inner need. So listen to your inner voice and tell your own versions of these stories. My wish is that you will embrace your coloring journey and ignite your passion for color.

—*Kinuko Y. Craft*

Colored by: _____   The Sea Dragon © Kinuko Y. Craft

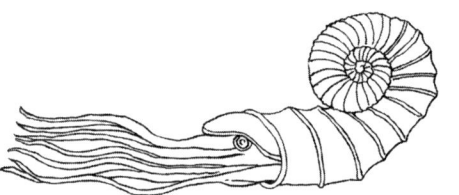

Colored by: Sunken City © Kinuko Y. Craft

Colored by: *Warrior Queen* © Kinuko Y. Craft

Colored by:

Eastern Vision © Kinuko Y. Craft

Colored by:

Inspiration © Kinuko Y. Craft

Colored by:

Huntress © Kinuko Y. Craft

Colored by:　　　　　　　　　　　　　　　　　　　　　　Nature Mandala © Kinuko Y. Craft

Colored by:

Dragon Dance © Kinuko Y. Craft

Colored by: *A Wet Kiss* © Kinuko Y. Craft

Colored by: _____   *Abundant Life* © Kinuko Y. Craft

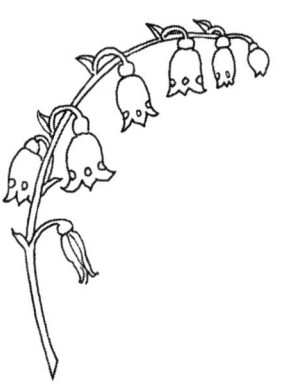

Colored by: Wild Reflection © Kinuko Y. Craft

Colored by: _____ Damselfly © Kinuko Y. Craft

Colored by: _____ A Dream of Orchids © Kinuko Y. Craft

Colored by:

Five Birds © Kinuko Y. Craft

Colored by: Claire's Wings © Kinuko Y. Craft

Colored by: _____   Unicorn © Kinuko Y. Craft

Colored by:

Byzantine Sanctuary © Kinuko Y. Craft

Colored by: For Beloved Wolf 832F © Kinuko Y. Craft

Colored by: Titania and Fish © Kinuko Y. Craft

Colored by: *Guardian* © Kinuko Y. Craft

Colored by:

Ancient Orient © Kinuko Y. Craft

Colored by: Beauty and the Beast © Kinuko Y. Craft

Colored by: Erato's Day Off © Kinuko Y. Craft

Colored by: 　　　　　　　　　　　　　　　　　　　　　　Winter Rose © Kinuko Y. Craft

Colored by: Still Life © Kinuko Y. Craft

Colored by:

Night Song © Kinuko Y. Craft

Colored by:

Starry Night © Kinuko Y. Craft

Colored by:　　　　　　　　　　　　　　　　　　　　　　　　　　　　　　Dragon Flies © Kinuko Y. Craft

Colored by: _____   Neptune's Daughter © Kinuko Y. Craft

Colored by: Sunrise Flowers © Kinuko Y. Craft

Colored by: Gryphon and Angel © Kinuko Y. Craft

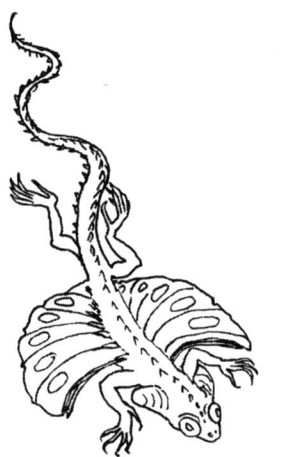

Colored by:　　　　　　　　　　　　　　Dragon, Phoenix, and Flying Lizard © Kinuko Y. Craft

Colored by: *Beloved* © Kinuko Y. Craft

Colored by: Leslie's Feather Tree © Kinuko Y. Craft

Colored by: Chinese Angel © Kinuko Y. Craft

Colored by:

Mask © Kinuko Y. Craft

Colored by: *Snow Sprite* © Kinuko Y. Craft

Colored by: *Flora* © Kinuko Y. Craft

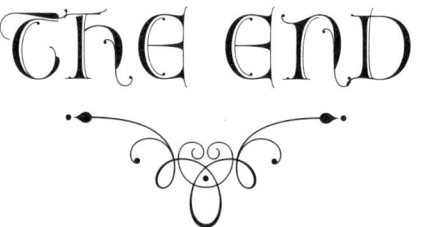

THE END

Colored by: *Dragonfly* © Kinuko Y. Craft